Reflections
in
Black and White

with

Shades of Red,
Yellow, and Brown

by
Gloria Gipson Suggs

DORRANCE PUBLISHING CO., INC.
PITTSBURGH, PENNSYLVANIA 15222

ISBN # 0-8059-3763-3
Printed in the United States of America

First Printing

For information or to order additional books, please write:
Dorrance Publishing Co., Inc.
643 Smithfield Street
Pittsburgh, Pennsylvania 15222
U.S.A.

Acknowledgment

The author wishes to thank Linda Suggs for sharing her talents in designing the graphics for this book. Thanks to Franklin, Michael, and Linda Suggs for their love, patience, suggestions, and encouragement.

Special thanks to my parents, Mr. and Mrs. S.P. Gipson, my sister, brothers, and the many friends and families of North Mississippi who helped to shape the way I view life in rural America.

To Franklin, Michael, and Linda

Contents

Introduction

Reflections in Black and White with Shades of Red, Yellow, and Brown is a child's poetic interpretation of the blending and bonding of families during the post-war years. It shows how situations and circumstances brought generations of families together, separated them, and eventually reunited them during political rallies, family reunions, and revivals.

Reflections in Black and White shows how a child dealt with the conflict and challenges of growing up and about the love and support received from extended and blended families during good and difficult times.

Reflections in Black and White with Shades of Red, Yellow, and Brown is divided into nine parts: "Walking in Big Shoes," "Walls Have Reflections Too," "A Different Point of View," "Love's Window," "Standing in Shadows," "Tall Thin Reflections Are Fun," "It's Revival Time," "Reunions of Reunions," and "Sing and Rap Some Songs for Me."

In *Reflections in Black and White*, the differences made the difference.

WALKING IN BIG SHOES

Gentle Reflections

Rooted heritage
On Big Papa's side
A tall handsome man
That sported a big stride
Gentle reflections
From Big Mama's face
Good bone structure
With hidden grace

Rooted heritage
From Big Papa's house
An indoor cistern
And a kitchen built to the south
Gentle reflections
From Big Mama's mirror
History embedded
In her living room's bureau

Rooted heritage
From Big Papa's shadow
He laid an educational guide
That will last tomorrow
Gentle reflections
Produced by Big Mama's love
Sent to rest in Heaven
On the wings of doves

I Can't Walk a Mile in Your Shoes

I haven't been broke and didn't have a dime
I haven't ever been moved to the back of the line
I haven't been lame
Nor have I been blind
I can't walk a mile in your shoes

I haven't felt the pain of hard time
I haven't ever stood in a welfare line
I haven't been abused
Nor have I been misused
I can't walk a mile in your shoes

I haven't been denied a job because of my race
I haven't been given one as a showcase
I haven't been homeless
Nor have I been nameless
I can't walk a mile in your shoes

Go Meet the Mail Man

Let me rest please
I am so tired
I have walked two miles to this road
I don't think the mail man has run yet
I would have heard his Model T Ford

Let me sit by the road, please
If the mail man comes, I will flag him down
I guess he will get here by noon
If he does, I can get home by One
He should be coming soon

Buckets of Spring Water

Go get one bucket of spring water
Spring water looks clear and clean
The best jellies and preserves are made with spring water
Spring water seems cooler than well water
Bring back two buckets of spring water

Go get three buckets of spring water
Spring water always tastes refreshing
Some people feel better after drinking spring water
Spring water seems clearer than cistern water
Bring back four buckets of spring water

Do You Remember that Day?

You made a vow and you kept it.
You found that dream house and you bought it.
You were offered a job and you took it.
Do you remember that day?

You earned big money and you saved it.
You hurt peoples' feelings but they forgave you.
You were lost and someone found you.
Do you remember that day?

You were assigned a task and you did it.
You made a debt but you paid it.
You set a goal and you reached it.
Do you remember that day?

If You Believe in Something

Look for it
Find it
Fight for it
Stand up for it
Go get it
Talk about it
Listen to it
Testify for it
Learn from it
Do it
Protect it
Wait for it
Trust in it
Speak up for it
Follow it
Work for it
Care for it
Treasure it

Reach high for it
Make it happen now

The Molasses Man

Spring rains are here
The soil is soft
When the weather clears
We'll clean the loft

Let's plant the sorghum on the hilly land
Where the sun shines brighter
And no trees will stand
The plants will grow taller
And we can strip them by hand
So the crop will be cleaner for the molasses man's cans

In summer, check the sorghum
Thin with need
If the canes are too close
The syrup won't be sweet
Check each plant for redness and roots for growth
It's the molasses man's job to taste the stalks

Well, fall is here
We've checked everything out
The mill is set up
The mules are stout
There he is, so proud of each can
That's Grandpa, the molasses man

These Three

These three are friends, you see
The preacher, the teacher, and Thee
Through good times and bad times
Through happy times and sad times
Together stand these three

These three make choices, you see
To preach, to teach, and to lead
The choices they make
are for our sake
The preacher, the teacher, and Thee

These three are pioneers you see
The preacher, the teacher, and Thee
In farming and education
Civil rights and salvation
They are known to you and me

These three go from place to place
To make sure all is well, you see
With deep devotion
Unwavering dedication
The preacher, the teacher, and Thee

This Tree

This tree stands so tall
It counts them coming in
And welcomes them all

This tree shelters from the sun and rain
Broad leaves spread wide
To comfort the tired and drained

This tree with roots standing high
Protects those "walking shoes"
For the people passing by

This tree marks the way
For buses to stop
And children to play

This tree says "Come on home"
To the wayward travelers,
Prodigal daughters and sons

This tree says it's okay
For all to come and go
But don't stay away

Stand Up and Shout

Stand up and shout if you want to
Ball up your fist and fight if you dare to
Take out a pen and write if you desire to
Statements are made that way

Go fly a kite if you want to
Burst a balloon if you'd like to
Wave a flag if you have a mind to
Statements are heard that way

Backward Motion

Moving backward will get you nowhere
Answering echoes is a waste of time
Looking away will confuse you
Frowning will make you old before your time
Backing up may even harm you
Writing backward is not a good sign
Some people told you during childhood
Backward motion could make you blind

A Dressed-up Lady

That lady all dressed up
Wearing a fancy hat
Trimmed in pink velvet
Matching her floral dress

Bright colors fit her well
Mixed with accents of gray
Set-off with embroidery
Trimmed in old lace

She has on high-top boots
Shined and tightly laced
The heels are not too high
She walks and moves with grace

She waves once or twice
Showing off her gloves
A fan in her right hand
Decorated with crepe myrtles

WALLS
HAVE REFLECTIONS TOO

Memories, Wind-blown

Memories, wind-blown
Stripped of shutters, tin, and paint
Tilting to the left
As I lose my upward reach
But oh, how I remember
Those days of yesteryear
When I was in my glory
And a major road passed by here

Memories, wind-blown?
No, people filled my rooms and stairs
For it was here they gathered
In birth, death, song, and prayer
Yes, my walls knew happy times
And loneliness I never felt
I enjoyed the hustle and bustle of people
And the sounds they always dealt

Memories, wind-blown?
Yes, that's what I am today
The sounds have gone
So have the people, oh so far away
Gone in all directions
Will they ever return?
I hope so
It's sad to be just memories, wind-blown

The Quilting Lamp

Sell me a good lamp to quilt by
I have pieced a four, eight, and sixteen patch
And started a Texas and a broken star
All the ladies will gather
At my house for supper
It will be very dark

Sell me a good lamp to quilt by
Let it match my Sunday china
Or pick up the flowers on the wall
The glow must be bright
So our stitches will be right
The shade should be tapered and tall

Don't Close the Kitchen Door

Canning will be done today
The kitchen is already hot
The windows are foggy
From the steamy dinner pot
Don't close the kitchen door

Corn, onions, and cabbages will be canned today
So will peaches, pears, and grapes
Potatoes and tomatoes will be canned tomorrow
With everything that bared late
So don't close that kitchen door

Pressure cookers will be whistling
A bumper crop was made this year
Jar lids will be popping
It will get very hot in here
Don't close that kitchen door

Tin Top Houses

It did not matter how small
There was still room for all

It did not matter how cold
The love inside warmed the soul

It did not matter how poor
Riches abound from giving more

It did not matter how dark the night
The lamp in the window seemed so bright

It did not matter how great
These humble dwellings kept you safe

It did not matter how long you were gone
When you came back, you were always welcomed home

Atway Store

Atway store
Don't close your door
We like your wood-burning heater
And hardwood floor

Atway store
Don't turn off your light
We want to see the throughway
And the turn to the right

Atway store
Don't run out of stock
We need soft drinks, candy,
And a pair of cotton socks

Grandma's Rocking Chair

We'll place it in the parlor next to the stair
Just to the left, please handle with care
All shiny and covered with fancy cloth
It's Grandma's rocking chair

We'll use it only when company comes
But if you are good, you may sit there
Still sturdy and strong after a hundred years
It's Grandma's rocking chair

We'll tell the stories of many children
Rocked to sleep with love and care
With gentle movements and songs so sweet
In Grandma's rocking chair

Let the Bucket Down

Let the bucket down, my son
Let the bucket down
I've been down here ever since one
Please let the bucket down

Let the bucket down, my child
Let the bucket down
I've been down here for a long while
Let the bucket down

Let the bucket down
Please let the bucket down
I don't want to be down here when they get from town
So, please let the bucket down

You Will Need These Things

You will need these things
When you move to your house
A wood-burning heater
and a heavy iron plow

You will need a flat bed wagon
A fertilizer and a hay rake
A heavy smoothing iron
And a pan in which to bake

21

Lye Soap

Lye soap was made from water, Mary War Lye, and hog fat
Mixed in a pot and boiled
Lye soap was cooked until the water left, cooled, and cut
Stored in brown paper coated with oil

Lye soap was used for washing clothes
Stained by dirt and grime
Lye soap made the wash come clean
And it didn't cost a dime

Big Red Truck

Big red truck, you came by here
We were all dressed up in shopping gear
We climbed your ladder, big and small
Grandma, Grandpa, families, and all
Your big wooden bed looked so tall
We had to hang on for fear we'd fall

Big red truck, you moved so fast
Through childhood and adulthood, we saw you pass
Pass the highways and byways on the way to town
You always had room for all around
From dusk to dawn you brought them all
Home, town, and back again—you never missed a call

Saturday's Shopping

Make a list of what you need
It's time for Saturday's shopping
Monday through Friday are school and work days
For reading, writing, and picking cotton

Sunday is going to church day
The stores in town will be closed
Merchants, deacons, preachers, and teachers
Will all be busy saving souls

Can't You Hear that Cotton Gin

Pick that cotton
Put it in the sack
Grab it fast
Bend your back
There is a race going on
Don't you want to win?
Can't you hear that cotton gin?

Five dollars to the winner
At the end of the day
For two hundred pounds gathered
What did you say?
You can spend it in town
For thread, cloth, paper, and pens
Can't you hear that cotton gin?

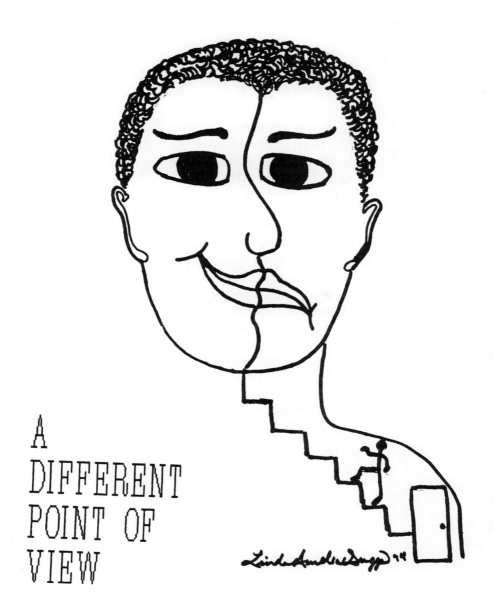

A
DIFFERENT
POINT OF
VIEW

That Ice Storm of '94

It came after midnight
In the form of frozen tears
Sparkling in the morning light
Like hanging chandeliers

Day by day the shapes appeared
From fallen trees and electric lines
It took us back to yesteryear
Reflecting scenes from the dawn of time

Was this nature's shrewd awakening
Or just a twist of fate
Was this a way of cleaning house
Revealing beauty in her wake

Old timers will keep talking
About bad weather seen before
Remembering in a second
That ice storm of '94

Good Luck Pieces

A horseshoe
Turned upside down
A guarantee
To turn your luck around

Two plow points
Turned toward the ground
A double dose
For ups and downs

A horseshoe
Hung over the door
A sure cure
For your fears and foes

Two plow points
Sprayed with gold
A guide for the young
And memories for the old

Shades

Shades of gray
sadden my day
and remind me that
a funeral is on the way

Shades of blue
my spirits renew
and I think of friends
loyal and true

Shades of green
make me feel good
about other people
and raises my self-esteem

Shades of red
remind me of Easter Eggs
and a big bunny rabbit
with a large bow on its head

Leaves

Leaves of trees change colors
Green, yellow, orange, red, and brown
Spring, summer, fall, and winter
Colors change all year round

Leaves of books are called pages
Torn, cut, folded, turned, short, medium, and long
Poetry, fiction, science, history
And music with words to songs

Leaves of time give breaks from work
Vacations, holidays, and sick leaves are clear
Tick-tock go the clocks
And bells ring in the new year

Seeds of Weeds

Seeds of weeds serve their purpose
Making waves on sands of time
Blending in with seeds of value
Tossed out if found in time

Seeds of weeds sprout with others
Holding back soil so fine
Bracing banks from rushing waters
Serving first on a firing line

Withstanding all types of weather
Producing blooms that blow the mind
Missing the chance to become a bouquet
Lasting years like vintage wine

This Little Lantern

This little lantern gave light
To gather the corn
To feed the hogs
To pickle the beets
And to cut the logs

This little lantern gave light
To hunt the opossums
To pick the chickens
To make lye soap
And to mend the mittens

This little lantern gave light
To nurse the babies
To cook the supper
To care for the sick
And to visit Big Mama and Big Papa

Milk and Bread Will Do

Cook a pan of corn bread
Make it crisp and brown
Put two eggs in it, please
Add a pinch of sugar, some butter milk, and Swan Down

Let it bake for fifteen minutes
Set aside to cool
Check to see if the milk has clabbered
Be sure the cream has been removed

Cut a piece of corn bread
Put it in a bowl
I'll take a cup of clabbered milk
I like mine fresh and cold

Let Me Tell Your Story Today

Let me tell your story today
Straight from Lucy's corner
I give the current news
From near, far, and yonder

Let me tell your story today
Straight from Phillip's school
I discuss visitations, illnesses, and recreations
When reporting Choulahoma's news

Let me tell your story today
I start with a friendly greeting
As you say it, I will send it in
Without hidden meanings

You Are Gonna Get a Whoppin' for That

You stole watermelons from your great-uncle's patch.
You broke a windowpane and you didn't put it back.
You let the cows get out and the hogs are not fat.
You are gonna get a whoppin' for that.

You visited all day instead of working till dawn.
You played every game when the adults were gone.
You rode the horse too fast and you drenched the cat.
You are gonna get a whoppin' for that.

You didn't wash the dishes or clean the house.
You forgot to get the eggs from the hayloft out.
You put on your Sunday clothes—shoes and hat.
You are gonna get a whoppin' for that.

Moving and Turning in Time

Swinging high
Swinging low
Walking past an open door
Sometimes fast
Sometimes slow
Moving and turning in time

Swaying left
Swaying right
Moving from the dark to light
Once day
Soon night
Moving and turning in time

Flying up
Diving down
Landing squarely on the ground
Fly high
Dive low
Moving and turning in time

LOVE'S WINDOW

If I Had Told You

If I had told you what you said would make me cry
Would you have gone away without saying good-bye?

If I had let you see the tears that stained my cheeks
Would you have stayed to comfort me?

If I had told you why I did not agree with you
Would you have listened to my point of view?

If I had told you about the sadness I felt inside
Would you have seen the burning tears in my eyes?

If I had told you only time would heal
Would you have shared the feelings you have felt for years?

Crying Alone Won't Cure Your Blues

Crying in crowds can be therapeutic
You can share the pain if you choose
Talking to others can be healthy
But crying alone won't cure your blues

Laughing alone is not so bad
Walking alone can be good for you
Dying alone is very sad
But crying alone will make you blue

We Did Not Know You

We did not know much about you
We wish we had
You used to come and visit
And relate the past

We did not see you every day
We missed you so
We heard many things about you
We loved you so

We did not listen
You tried to tell
Why we resembled you
And you always wished us well

Love Thoughts

Come and linger awhile, my love
Come and watch me while I laugh because I am so happy
With all your faults, I love you
With all your dreams, I admire you

God is a wonderful God
I guess every person who is in love
Or ever hopes to be in love
Knows this by now

Sure, there will come sorrow
Yes, there will come pain
But because God is with us always
We shall overcome
And we shall see the day when we can be together forever

Southeast County Line

We'll meet there right at midnight
Or just about a quarter to nine
What will they say
About us meeting this way
At that southeast county line

The moon beams will act as guide posts
Or treasures for lovers to find
Will they miss us when
Dusk comes again
At that southeast county line

Look for me in the shadows
Between the grove of slender pines
We will run away
and marry by day
Down at that southeast county line

I Would Help You If I Could

You move so slowly and you seem unsure
You reach for things that aren't there
Sometimes a glass or a rocking chair
You want to go home because you feel you should
I would help you if I could

You speak so softly and unsure
You call for help but no one hears
Sometimes in shouts followed by tears
You try to do things that others would
I would help you if I could

Those Wash Board Blues

Sheets hanging on the line
Socks bleaching in the tub
Linens boiling in the number thirty pot
Quilts drying on the shrubs
Lingerie soaking in the wash pan
A new type of blueing just made the news
Rubbing, ranging, shaking, hanging
I think I got those wash board blues

Rocking Alone

The blues come in different ways
All at once or one by one
Overpowering and then some
But none so blue as rocking alone

Some call it depression
Others call it longing for home
Back and forth the blues will get you
If you are caught rocking alone

Quilted Diamonds

Quilted diamonds
Cut from cloth
Expressed my feelings
And inner thoughts

Quilted diamonds
I stitched the first
Which centered the love
For our children's births

Quilted diamonds
Forming rings
Composed of scraps
From dresses and things

Quilted diamonds
Attached with care
Will forever endure
Through sickness and health

Quilted diamonds
Our love did bind
Increased in value
A million times

Love in a Different Light

You look so different each time I see you
Smiles—frowns—laughter—tears
Or just a look of afterthought
Walking—running—singing—humming
Or wearing the birthday present I last bought
Turning left or looking right
Old or young
Weak or strong
Each time I see you,
I love you in a different light

Money Matters

All you want to do is talk about money
That's the last thing on my mind
All you want to discuss is money matters
Money matters waste my time

All you think about is money
Money! Money! Yours or mine
Your paycheck was short by a hundred dollars
Money matters are making us blind

I Know About My Roses

I know about my roses
I tend them every day
I cut out the weeds and undergrowth
So nothing is in their way

I know about my roses
I watch them one by one
I pray that God may keep them
As they go and come

I know about my roses
I count them every day
There were sixteen when I checked last
Did one or two go away?

I know about my roses
God has blessed them one and all
I come each day in a very quiet way
Just in case they slip and fall

Who Sees the Beauty

Who sees the beauty of nature?
Is it the person who walks by moonlight
in a trance defined as love?
Is it the child who feels its mother's tears
warm against its cheeks?
Or could it be the blind man
who captures the glow of the sun in a dream
and hears the gushing of a wind-blown lake?

Who sees the beauty of nature?
Are there special beings
who have been endowed with this rare gift?
Or is this rare gift
something that has been instilled in all living things?
Who amongst us can really testify to the depth
and warmth of nature's rare beauty
and reveal to all the hidden secrets of it?

Winter's Sights and Sounds

Squirrels scrambling up a tree
Black birds chirping at things they see
People rushing in the snow and rain
Shrubs frozen against window panes
Rabbits running all around
These are winter's sights and sounds

Potatoes roasting in the fireplace
Tables set with stoneware and old lace
Smokestacks seen from afar
Icicles hanging from the bottom of a car
Lakes frozen up and down
These are winter's sight and sounds

Baking yeast bread and serving wine
Up at dawn and to bed by nine
Children playing in the snow
Lovers kissing under missile toe
People rushing into town
These are winter's sights and sounds

STANDING IN SHADOWS

Release those Shackles and Chains

You are all tied up in a knot
Complaining about your aches and pains
You lost your job last week
So now you can't pay the man
Your wife left you last year
A storm blew out all the window panes
Stop complaining
Release those shackles and chains

Your car was stolen last night
You lost your last dime
The mailbox is full of doctor bills
Bad luck is messing up your mind
Your best friend told some lie on you
So you missed your chance at fame
Get a life
Release those shackles and chains

Wasted fuel

Wasted fuel and broken fences
Uncut weeds and overturned benches

Incomplete deeds and forgotten promises
Shattered dreams and dried-up vintages

Hindered growth and mingled thoughts
Far-flung hopes and forgotten folks

Burned bridges and tangled wires
Blocked doorways and sad good-byes

Confusion

Rocking and rolling
Rumbling and mumbling
Fussing and cussing
Shucking and jiving
Confusion

Pushing and shoving
Banging and bumping
Hitting and missing
Tooting and looting
Confusion, confusion

Shaking and breaking
Stopping and stumbling
Twisting and twirling
Whisking and whirling
Confusion, confusion, confusion

Bossy Lady

Sit down, girl.
Close your mouth and listen.
Don't talk so much.
Get some water from the cistern.

Come here, girl.
Pick these turnip greens.
Did you shell some peanuts?
Don't be so mean.

Wake up, girl.
Don't forget to feed the chicken.
Did you milk the cow?
Did you paint the kitchen?

Life's Ups and Downs

I have difficulty understanding life
Things and people are always moving so fast
And sometimes things hurt so deeply

In figuring out life, I place things such as hate, despair,
love, pain, and patience at the top of my list
because these are the most difficult for me to understand

But problems are solved every day.
So why can't these things be understood by me?
I know they can be solved, but how?

A Child in Despair

I can't go on like this
All weighted down with problems
Not knowing how I will make it from day to day
I have thought about running away
But where would I go?
Who would I call once I get there?

I can't go on anymore
Nothing I do is right
When I laugh, it is always too loud
When I talk, it is always in the wrong tone of voice
I can't go on anymore
I feel like a stranger lost in a crowd

Somebody

Somebody blocked the way
To the voting booth that day
They went through town
Then two miles around
Somebody walked away

The rain poured down
On the way through town
To the voting booth they say
When the ballots were cast
Somebody shouted that day

Situations and Opportunities

Have you ever been lonely and met a friend?
Did you lose something twice and find it again?
Did you do something in honest that some called a crime?
Situations and opportunities are like that sometimes.

Have you seen a falling star and made a wish that came true?
Did you go to a surprise party someone planned for you?
Did you miss a bargain because you didn't have the fee?
Opportunities and situations come and go like that, you see.

Have you ever helped a stranger who had lost his way?
Did you think something was blue when it really was gray?
Did you make a wrong turn on a road you knew?
Situations and opportunities like these are few.

Four Walls

Four walls will not hold you
If you really want to go
Four no's cannot stop you
From reaching your own guidepost

Four winds will not change your course
If you have carefully planned your way
Four gates will not lock you in
And make you lose the race

Four lies won't stop you
When choosing friends afar and few
Let them serve as warnings
When old walls pass for new

Four falls will slow you down
and make you a little unsure
Four yes's will encourage you
To climb walls and open doors

TALL THIN REFLECTIONS
ARE FUN

That Bushy Tail Cat

That bushy tail cat is too fat
Some say she is downright lazy
She sleeps all day
At night she plays
Some say that bushy tail cat is crazy

That bushy tail cat wears my hat
And sleeps on my shoes
She opens doors
When she sleeps she snores
That bushy tail cat looks at the news

That bushy tail cat acts like a spoiled brat
She leaves the house for days
She hides in the attic
Climbs a door in panic
That bushy tail cat has funny ways

That bushy tail cat is a very good pet
She sits on a mat and listens to me chat
She likes bird watching but she hates the word "scat"
She has golden eyes and fur that's jet black
You will like that bushy tail cat

A Ghost Called Moe

A ghost called Moe lives in our house
He bumps coming in
He squeaks going out
Sometimes we mistake him for a mouse
Moe is a noisy ghost

A ghost called Moe moves swiftly through our house
He throws things around
He makes whirlwind sounds
Look out!
Moe is a dangerous ghost

A ghost called Moe does pranks at night
He jumps around
and moves quickly out of sight
Sometimes he changes from dim to bright
Moe is an elusive ghost

Tell about that Honky-tonk

Once there was a Honky-tonk
Way back off the road
It was a different kind of Honky-tonk
At least that's what was told
People came to this Honky-tonk
Just to have fun
On Fridays right at sundown
That Honky-tonk was always full

There was always dancing at that Honky-tonk
To Blues, Country, and Rock-n-Roll
The Twist, the Square Dance, the Electric Slide
Some even danced the Stroll

The fish fries started at sun down
They fried Salmon—Catfish—Perch
Whiten—Buffalo—and Trout
That fish tasted so good

Some people called it a night spot
And some called it a country club
As imagined by a child—some will agree
That was a special kind of Honky-tonk

Back Porch Talk

Did you hear about that man
From down yonder's way
He left town last night
At least that's what they say

He was too friendly with the ladies
That made the folks real mad
So they asked him to leave town
They talk like he was pretty bad

He gave one lady a gold necklace
He gave her best friend some pearls
He sent some lady a long fur coat
At least that is what I heard

Some men are good and honest
Some move from place to place
Some hide behind fancy clothes
Just to save face

Under the China Berry Trees

Toys and doll houses
Mud pies and songs
Running and swinging
Tagging along
Hide-n-Seek and watching the bees
Under the China Berry Trees

Bicycles and wagons
Marbles and jacks
Whistling and wresting
And racing in potato sacks
These are special memories
Under the China Berry Trees

My Dog Named Lady

Lady, Lady
My special Lady
A special Lady who protects my home
She has class
So I don't get mad
When she digs up the garden to hide her bones

Lady, Lady
My loyal Lady
She stands beside me when I'm right and wrong
A true friend
Through thick and thin
She runs down the street tagging me along

Lady, Lady
My playful Lady
She runs after birds and the bees
Turns turtles on their backs
Barks at the cat
And chases squirrels up a tree

That Fishing Pond

Let's get our canes at just about dawn
And go down to that fishing pond

We'll leave the fields when the work is done
And catch some fish from that fishing pond

Let's tell the other children, it'll be such fun
We might take a swim in that fishing pond

The adults won't mind, the cool winds have come
They might go with us to that fishing pond

Let's be real quiet and place our hooks toward the sun
So we'll catch plenty of fish from that fishing pond

IT'S REVIVAL TIME

Come On, Mourner

Come on mourner and join the army
The sermons are fiery and the hymns have harmony
We'll pray and sing all night if there is hope for you
Come on, mourner—join the army

You have been on the mourner's bench
Every day since Monday
Two preachers have preached
One came down with hoarseness
It's Friday night
Baptizing is Sunday
There were seven mourners at the start of revival
Six have confessed
You are the only one left
Now is the time for you to join the rest

Come on mourner and join the army
It's just about midnight and time for the benediction
We'll sing one more song and pray one more prayer
Please, come on, mourner, we're tired, sleepy, and hungry

You Sound Like a Preacher

You start with the Old
And end with the New
You open and close service with a hymn or two
Restating your text as the spirit moves you
You sure were called to preach
And you speak properly
You sound like a preacher to me

You talk of trials and tribulations
With the patience of Job
Relating events to the salvation of souls
You talk to the young about those pearly gates of gold
Asking for an Amen from the deacons—now and then
You wave to the sisters as they shout and wave their hands
You sound and look like a preacher to me

Your voice gets high and low
When bringing home a point
You pray in a whisper
Sometimes long—sometimes short
You strut back and forth—humming for awhile
When the congregation shouts, you end your text
Sounding just like a preacher

Evil Spirits

Don't let evil spirits get to you
Some are old and some are new
Some wear smiles, some wear frowns
Some will pick you up
Some will only let you down

Don't let evil spirits come your way
Some come at night and some by day
Some are bold and some are shy
Some are talkative
Others are very quiet

Don't let evil spirits block your view
Some move back and forth in front of you
Some turn lights on and off
Some flash stained glass signs
Don't let evil spirits make you stop

Don't let evil spirits take charge of your life
Some are black and some are white
Some come in many shades of red, yellow, and brown
Don't let evil spirits get in your way
Or get you down

A Song Leader Called Sang

She was tall and large in structure
To some she looked rather plain
She sung in a deep voice
She never got hoarse
A song leader called Sang

She lead songs that everyone knew
They all had standard refrains
A favorite song
That was not too long
Lead by a song leader called Sang

She would stop and drink some water
From a jug next to the pew
She would pick the song up
At the right verse
That song leader everybody knew

No one knew much about her
Or the place from which she came
But they remember the words
And the contralto voice heard
From the song leader called Sang

I Can Ring Those Church Bells

I can't sing the song you gave me
I can't pick peaches from the trees
Finding my way around this place
Sometimes can be a task for me
I sure can't get honey from bees
But I can ring those church bells

I am too short to erase the backboard
I am too small to lace my own shoes
Making clothes is out of the question
I am too young to vote
That bag is too big for me to tote
But I can ring those church bells

I can't make Children's Day speeches
I am afraid to lead that song
I can say The Lord's Prayer
But not out loud
I am downright afraid of crowds
I can ring those church bells

Let the Piano Man Play

Let the piano man play those songs
Let the piano man play
Although a little out of key
They don't sound so bad
They make the spirit come over me
Let the piano man play

Sometimes he plays different sounds
A little jazz—a little rock
You might hear some blues
But when you hear those gospel notes
You will feel the holy ghost
Let the piano man play

He gets up and struts around
He sits down—he stands up
Then he sits back down and plays
He sings good too
Let the spirit have its way
Let the piano man play

Communion Day

From an open window, I was greeted by the brightest sunrise.
Even the birds sounded different to me.
The people I met on this day seemed more light-hearted.
The grass appeared a darker green on this day.
The flowers seemed to have taken on a sweeter fragrance.

That evening, the sun disappeared behind a grove of pine trees.
Only red and yellow beams were revealed after it.
It was the most wonderful sight I have ever seen.
This day started well and ended well.
And I was happy.

REUNIONS OF REUNIONS

They Keep Coming

They keep coming
Some by cars
Some by trains
Some in suits
And some in jeans

They keep coming
From the oceans
From the mountain
From the beaches
And from the plains

They keep coming
From the North
From the South
From the East
And from the West

They keep coming
United by common goals and dreams
Hearing the ancestral call
To the family reunions
Grandpa, Grandma, and all

When Grandma Comes to Visit

When Grandma comes to visit
Be on your best behavior
Hang up your clothes
Polish your shoes
Cook a cake with vanilla flavor

When Grandma comes to visit
Stack the logs next to the fence
Cut the grass
Water the flowers
Plant some zinnias and green mints

When Grandma comes to visit
Sweep the floors
Wash the dishes
Do the laundry
Clean the dust off the pictures

Forty Acres and a Mule

When they got their papers
Stating they were free
Generations of bonded brothers
Shouted out with glee
Some felt it did not matter
As long as they were free
They were given a mule and forty acres
And forty dollars to buy some seeds

North they went looking for fortune
East and west—for fame
South they went seeking shelter
And to see a familiar face
They were bonded together as brothers
For generations or two
They united again as brothers
Forty acres and a mule didn't do

They united again as brothers
Forty acres and a mule didn't do

Grandma's Flower Garden Still Looks Good

Sunflowers act as backdrop
Daisies fill in the middle
Petunias serve as border plants
For easy watering with a kettle

Zinnias stand in-between
The Red Irises and Blue Tulips
Pink Crepe Myrtle near the house
Serve as shade for the ferns

Primroses on the picket fence
Yellow Cactus in a tub
Some Four O'clock just sprouted out
Behind the chimney next to the wood

Some Marigolds are in full bloom
Purple Tulips just opened up
A trench around a Formosa tree
Contains budding Buttercups

The Morning Glories look real good
Beneath that red Hibiscus
The Magnolia tree is in full bloom
On the porch sat a bucket of White Carnations

Those Mother-in-Law Tongues are holding their own
So are the Bird-in-the-Nest
The Sweet Williams came up again
The Yellow Mums will be next

That Dogwood tree in the corner
Still supports those Honeysuckle vines
That Mulberry tree still is home for the bees
And the Cedar trees are doing just fine
Grandma's flower garden still looks good

Turnip Greens Don't Taste Bad

Pick them
Snap them
Soak them
Shake them
Wash them
Rinse them
Wring them
Would you bake some corn bread?
Peel them
Slice them
Boil them
Season them
Simmer them
Cool them
Eat them
Turnip greens don't taste bad!

Time to Catch that Train

Lend me some money to buy a ticket
I'll pay you back next week
My son is going to Chicago
The train is leaving at eight

His bags are packed and ready
To catch a ride to town
He worked in the fields yesterday
Until about sundown

Don't worry about your money
He will send it to me soon
He has a job waiting in Chicago
He got the news at noon

He will stay with relatives in Chicago
Just outside of Champaign
They will be moving back home next year
On that south-bound train

74

SING AND RAP SOME
SONGS FOR ME

Linda Amlin Duggs

America, You Are on the Go

VERSE 1

America, you're on the go
From sea to sea and shore to shore
North, south, east, and west
America, you're moving fast

VERSE 2

America, you're looking good
From southern plains to northern woods
Mountain tops, rivers, and lakes
America, you're looking great

CHORUS

America
The beautiful
Land of the free
Your mountain tops and rolling plains
You look so good to me

VERSE 3

America, you're on the move
Building homes, churches, and schools
To every child, woman, and man
America, you're lending a hand

VERSE 4

America, you're doing fine
Cleaning up and solving crime
Providing food and jobs for the poor
America, you are opening doors

CHORUS

America, the beautiful
Land of the free
Your mountain tops and rolling plains
You look so good to me

You look so good to me
You look so good to me

Teams in the Southeast

VERSE 1

Organize
Energize
Motivate
Advertise
Are the goals of progressive teams in the southeast
Show and tell
Listen well
Seek them out
Treat them swell
Are the themes of progressive teams in the southeast

VERSE 2

Plant the seeds
Let them grow
Share the fruits
For all to know
Are the goals of progressive teams in the southeast
Plant more seeds
Shine more light
Add some fuel
Let them thrive
Are the themes of progressive teams in the southeast

CHORUS

Organize
Energize
What a difference you have made in the southeast
Listen well
Show and tell
Thank you for a job well done in the southeast

Preserves, Jellies, and Jams

Make me some jellies and jams, my child
Make me some jellies and jams
Preserves are good
But I wish you would
Make me some jellies and jams

Jellies and jams taste good, my child
Jellies and jams taste good
I remember them
From way back when
Finger licking jellies and jams

Jellies and jams will do, my child
Jellies and jams will do
Preserves are fine
But on my mind
Are biscuits, jellies, and jams

Jellies and jams
Jellies and jams
I like jellies and jams
Preserves are fine
But on my mind
Are Grandma's jellies and jams

Steep Is the Stairway to Heaven

CHORUS

Steep is the stairway to Heaven
I'm tired, but I want my crown
With Jesus at my side
It doesn't seem so high
I'm moving to higher ground

Verses

1. I'm marching this journey so slowly
I feel the pains of time
Jesus comforts me
Steps I clearly see
For nothing can stop my climb

2. Step by step, I'm climbing the stairway
I walk with my hand in thine
With Jesus as my guide
I feel so satisfied
How brightly my pathway shines

3. Alone, I'm not for this moment
Jesus hears my every cry
So safe I feel
For it is his will
I'll complete my journey now

I Feel the Presence of God

CHORUS

I feel the presence of God
I feel the presence of God
Both day and night
When I'm wrong or right
I feel the presence of God

1. When things go wrong and fill me with doubt
The road seems so rough like there is no way out
I remember the grace that brought me this far
And I feel the presence of God.

2. When each day confronts me with life's broken dreams
And unreachable goals are so far unseen
Oh how amazing the voice that calls
And I feel the presence of God

3. Whenever I'm lost in life's rushing waves
Dim is the light that leads me astray
I see the glow from a distant state
And I feel the presence of God

This Makes Me Realize

So high is the mountain
So vast is the sky
So deep is His valley
This makes me realize how Great God is

So blue is His ocean
So bright is His sun
So green is His pasture
This makes me realize how Great God is

So swift is His lightning
So mighty is His storm
So gusty is His billow
This makes me realize how Great God is

Beyond the Sky

CHORUS

Christ paid the price
Christ paid the price
For the right to the tree of life
Low is the way
And rough is the journey
To that home beyond the sky

VERSES

1. Low is the way
And rough the journey
To that place where storms don't rise
Christ gave His life
To assure salvation
In that home beyond the sky

2. Small is the crowd
And few the faithful
To the city where sun always shines
So Christ gave His life
As confirmation
To that home beyond the sky

3. Dark is the night
And death shows no mercy
In that valley where souls seek to rise
So Christ beamed his light
To show direction
To that home beyond the sky

The Blood of The Lamb

CHORUS

The blood of The Lamb
Oh, the blood of The Lamb
Cleanse our souls in the blood of The Lamb
The blood of the Lamb
Oh, the blood of The Lamb
Save us in the blood of The Lamb

VERSES
1. Wash our souls in the blood of the Lamb
Fill our hearts with love and grace
Guide our feet in the path of righteousness
Save us in the blood of The Lamb

2. Take our hands in times of doubt and fear
Prepare our hearts for many hurts and pains
Cleanse our minds from thoughts of earthly greed
Save us in the blood of The Lamb

What Light, Assuring Light

1. What Light, Assuring Light
Comes from the Son of God
What Light, Assuring Light
Outshines the brightest star
What Light, Assuring Light
Guides us near and oh so far
What Light
Oh What Light
What Assuring Light

2. What Light, Assuring Light
Comforts in times of grief
What Light, Assuring Light
Knows our every need
What Light, Assuring Light
Our hungry souls do feed
What Light
Oh What Light
What Assuring Light

3. What Light, Assuring Light
Sends Amazing Grace
What Light, Assuring Light
Receives the highest praise
What Light, Assuring Light
God sends to prepare our way
What Light
What Light
What Assuring Light

Faith, Hope, and Charity

CHORUS

Faith, hope, and charity
Taught the Man that died for me
Charity, love, and peace
Taught the Man from Galilee

VERSES

1. Faith—in the Man who died
Hope—because He shed his blood
Charity, love and peace
Taught the Man who died for me
Faith—keeps us hanging on
Hope—cleanses hearts from wrong
Charity, love, and peace
Taught the Man from Galilee

2. Faith—in the Holy Word
Hope—because He shed His blood
Charity, love, and peace
Taught the Man who died for me
Faith—shows us the way
Hope—guides us night and day
Charity, love and peace
Taught the Man from Galilee

3. Faith—takes us through the night
Hope—makes our future bright
Charity, love, and peace
Taught the Man who died for me
Faith—in the heavenly home
Hope—makes us strong
Charity, love and peace
Taught the Man from Galilee

God Makes Everything Alright

The sun refuses to shine
The day becomes as night
Temptation blocks our minds
Confuses wrong with right
All faith in men is gone
God makes everything alright

The family structure fails
Sisters and brothers at war
The churches no longer prevail
Sermons aren't heard anymore
Men seek fortune and fame
God makes everything alright

Our names are blemished with shame
So-called friends are gone
Our earthly bodies fail
We seem so all alone
God makes every thing alright

You Took the Time

1. You took the time, Lord
To show us the way
Precious, precious time
So we would not stray
You took the time, Lord
To brighten our day
Thank you, Lord Jesus Christ

2. You took the time, Lord
To die on the cross
Precious, precious time
So we would not fall
You took the time, Lord
To hear our call
Thank you, Dear Jesus Christ

3. You took the time, Lord
To hear our cry
Precious, precious time
To suffer and die
You took the time, Lord
So trouble won't rise
Thank you, Lord Jesus Christ

Oh Such a Beautiful Day

CHORUSES

1. Oh such a beautiful day
In that greater by and by
Oh such a beautiful day
In that home beyond the sky
Such a beautiful day
Such a beautiful day
With friends and family
Oh such a beautiful day
Prepared for you and me

2. Oh such a beautiful day
When the glory of Christ shall rise
Fear of death won't come our way
So dry your weeping eyes
Oh what great confirmation
Christ lived, suffered, and died
Oh such a beautiful day
In that greater by and by

VERSES

1. It's gonna be a beautiful day
Rejoicing there will be
Singing songs of praise
With friends and family
Oh such a beautiful day
Made for you and me

2. It's gonna be a beautiful day
When the glory of Christ shall rise
Fear of death won't come our way
So dry your weeping eyes
Oh such a beautiful day
In that greater by and by